BLUE RAIN

GAVIN GOODWIN

INDEPENDENT INNOVATIVE INTERNATIONAL

Published by Cinnamon Press
Meirion House
Tanygrisiau
Blaenau Ffestiniog
Gwynedd
LL41 3SU
www.cinnamonpress.com

The right of Gavin Goodwin to be identified as author of this work has been asserted by him in accordance with the Copyright, Designs and Patent Act, 1988. Copyright © 2018 Gavin Goodwin.
ISBN: 978-1-910836-93-4
British Library Cataloguing in Publication Data. A CIP record for this book can be obtained from the British Library.
Designed and typeset in Palatino by Cinnamon Press.
Cover design by Jan Fortune.
Printed in Poland
Cinnamon Press is represented in the UK by Inpress Ltd and in Wales by the Welsh Books Council

Acknowledgements

Some of these poems (or earlier versions of them) have appeared in the following publications: *Agenda, Agenda Broadsheets, GeoHumanities, Glimmer and other stories and poems* (Cinnamon, 2011), *Poetry Wales, Word~River: Literary Review, Writing Urban Space* (Zero, 2012)

With thanks to John Freeman, and the Aberystwyth Poetry Group: Neal Alexander, Peter Barry, Matt Jarvis, Creina and Matthew Francis, Richard Marggraf-Turley. And special thanks, as always, to my wife, Reina.

Contents

for my parents

Blue Rain

The Greenhouse Effect

Between the two cities, in huge greenhouses,
where wages are paid
       for weight, not time,

we sweat, doubled-over, one to a cart—
twisting tomatoes
       at speed from the vine.

Each morning we wake, our tailbones burning
and rise, graceless,
       into the dark.

The economy's growing, the radio says.
We bow again
       under the glass.

Dam Quatrains

we travel   enclosed   by ice-carved hills
these seemingly still   Silurian rocks
the first scuttle   and blossom of life
on land beside   beyond the water

a land mined   since caligae trod here
by thirty-three   those men were dead   we see
poison   leak from the tailing   river
still swimming   with copper and lead

bowed by wind   the valley trees
follow the water   back to its source
black peat   gravel and heather
bog origin—Ystwyth and Elan

iron-stained strata   rust-coloured cascade
the eddy and swirl   of pebbles slowly
burrow down   into the bedrock
burrow with ever-   refreshing force

vertigo   follow   the rippling sheet
of cloud pouring   down from the lake
pouring in   to the giant holding
tank from which   a city will drink

cold's now   set in my feet   no stamping
or rubbing it out   hunger   mist
floats up from the falls   and a turbine spins
        light from the force

measure that pick   against that dam
and understand   his stone stoop
in green silence   his back turned
to the white force   the froth and thunder

we travel back—light over Aber
last light   of the short day   Ystwyth
pouring   into the harbour
waves   stones   change in the dusk

Winter Horses

Almost blind, she leaves the low rise,
knapsack stretched across her back,

and slow-walks the narrow lanes.
They are waiting.

                    Door sealed
shut with ice. She pulls hard to crack it,

enters the caravan, strikes a match.
Before the kettle blows,

she unlocks the wooden stable—
their breath   their warmth
                  charging the dark.

No Brutalist School

no waffle slab ceilings suspended
above us—a showroom of bathtubs

capsized   no stalactites glisten
no pansies are dwarfed

by octagon pots of concrete
no slap of a ball on the green-cork gym

no wall of glass to swelter behind
no gelled parting, no bruise like a leech

swelling under your eye   no swapping
of tapes and dreams   no writing in rows

no skulking over the pitches
in the muddy, melting snow

no roof water drains to a straightened stream
no boy in kayak is turning to camera

for *Design* magazine on opening day:
no *minor, if slightly flawed, masterpiece*

Unloved and derided locally…
seen as a liability

no diggers roll in to gouge out the classrooms
leaving a tangle of stiff steel veins

just this flattened stretch of mud, speckled
with Forticrete grey   a square of water

brown and still   and two geese circling

For Idle Hands

He kneels in
the walk-in fridge,
breathing
pink detergent.

His fingers work,
wet and numb,
beneath the towers of meat.

He plunges,
with slow relief,
his hands
into the cooling fryer

and wears two,
still-warm
gloves of yellow fat.

Walking home
on heavy limbs,
he burns
through a cigarette.

In gloam
from the hedgerow —
a panicked scratching.

He stops, peers,
reaches in,
pulls back
the prickled branches.

A thrush slips
free and lifts
above the wires and rooftops.

Blue Rain

a trio of abandoned vans
drop rust along the carpark

behind them   an empty house
is going up in flames

    and out we pour
    into the night

    among the smoke
    and rumours

brigade arrive in Nomex
with hoses of blue rain

at first light   each van
wears a damp skin of ash

behind them   the silent
house throbs like a wound

The Ballad of Ronan Point

Later today you'll find our names
in the paper, they'll be on the list.

Later today you'll find our names
on the list of those missing.

I was on   the 18th floor.
I never turned any gas on
at all—just filled the kettle up
and was thrown on the floor.

About 5.15 we heard
a terrific explosion.
The next thing we know,
half the building's falling down.

We just panicked, up and ran,
knocking doors along the veranda.
One woman just about scrambled back
into bed as the lot fell.

Later today you'll find our names

I knew we were going to find bad workmanship—
what surprised me was the sheer scale of it.
Not a single joint was correct. Fixing
straps were unattached: levelling
nuts were not wound down   joints
      within the structure,
      filled with newspapers
      rather than concrete.

17

in the paper, they'll be on the list

A number of people jumped the fences
and ran into the building.
We managed to get to the third floor,
I think, and brought down
an elderly, bedridden lady
who was living on her own apparently
and the gentleman who was with me,
I don't know his name unfortunately,
carried her onto an ambulance
and I went back …

Later today you'll find our names

On the same day that engineers
told the enquiry
that they feared for the safety
of thousands of residents,

Taylor Woodrow-Anglian
and Newham Council convened
a special Press Conference
to announce

that two more blocks
had been completed
and would be occupied
immediately.

on the list of those missing

You want to get out
of these rotten slums.
We've got to build
the accommodation
necessary for you.

Here it is,
        on the doorstep
and that's all
we can offer you.

hanging down ceilings
layered like lizard scales

        'Homes must
        not be wasted'

In Waves

early   drive   the city frays
fields   threads
          of motorway

the spread of fog grows thin toward
the sea
          the sun is rising

the sound of wave
on wave   moving

through a shifting
          floor of pebbles

through the ear's
canal of bone

sense   the heart is slowing

and enter now the calm sea   gasp deep
into the cold
          water folds – sun lit
waiting for
          the shock to pass

still the pebbles, plastics move
smooth misted discs of glass

the waves are black
and beating

against the high
sea wall

along
the southern beach

a bank of foam
is rippling

yellow in
the lamp light

the tumbleweeds
of froth

walking   suppressing
a hope for grace
you enter
              or become

a spaciousness
waves
      thoughts   allowed
            to pass

along the gravel path
     conifers   felled
cold wind   cliff
  bracken full of bells

waves slap the wetsuit legs   casting
nets of kelp around them
                    place your board
into the surf, flop your weight across it

duck dive, as you were taught, cold splinters
through the skull
                    and paddle past the breakers,
to where the mackerel swim

with mercury in their blood   a swell starts
to carry you in
                    unbalanced you go under, unsure
which way is up …

washed upon the beach
deflated   still

at touch of water
this brainless body

clarifies   takes on
the darkness of sand

as sea drains back
this bloodless jelly

fills with a mist of light

sat crossed-legged on your board   paddle placed
before you   grey stones
                           pass below you
the water   bright
you drift across the bay

gratitude arising
                      unbidden as a wave

Bottlenose

Fifty-two million
years since returning

to sea and beginning
the slow smoothing

of feet into fins
the waves removing

the hair from your flesh
an airway climbing

away from your face
echolocating, leaving

a slight smile in its wake

and now you are sliding
up through the surface

and now leaping
a dark and glimmering

arc in the air
a liquid motion

the ripples passing
through us for days.

Notes

'No Brutalist School' features quotations from: Alistair Best, 'Newport High's Low Profile', *Design*, 292 (1970) and from Jon Wright, 'Newport High School', May 2008, in *Twentieth-Century Society: Casework and Campaigns*.

'The Ballad of Ronan Point' features (often modified) quotations from: '1968: Three Die as Tower Block Collapses', *On This Day 1950-2005*. BBC News; Patrick Dunleavy, *The Politics of Mass Housing in Britain, 1945-1975: A Study of Corporate Power and Professional Influence in the Welfare State* (Oxford: Clarendon Press, 1981) and Cynthia Rouse and Norbert Delatte, 'Lessons from the Progressive Collapse of the Ronan Point Apartment Tower', in *Forensic Engineering: Proceedings of the Third Conference*, ed. by Paul A. Bosela, Norbert J. Delatte, and Kevin L. Rens (San Diego: American Society of Civil Engineers, 2003) and Dominic Gallagher, 'Ronan Point', OpenLearn<http://www.open.edu/openlearn/history-the-arts/history/heritage/ronan-point>

All quotations used with kind permission of the authors or sources quoted.